Black Fox Literary
M A G A Z I N E

Black Fox Literary Magazine is a print and online literary magazine published biannually.

Issue 19 Cover Art: *Vive La Resistance* by Letisia Cruz

ISBN: 978-1-7336240-3-9

Editors' Note

What a privilege to be writing to you after all this time away. Without getting into too much detail, 2019 was a rough year for us. We tried hard to keep things going and even read submissions during that time, but at last, something had to give. We've said it before, this magazine has and always will be a labor of love. This very fact is what has allowed us to bring it back. As we mentioned on social platforms, the work we do is too important to give up on. Ultimately, helping writers get their work out and be heard is too important.

We are writing this during the time of the Coronavirus pandemic. If there's anything this situation has taught us, it's that more than ever we need writers. Their words help us cope, entertain us, and help us heal. So, we leave you with one takeaway: don't stop creating. Don't stop telling your stories. The world needs you.

-The Editors
Racquel, Pam, and Marquita

Meet the *BFLM* Staff:

Founding Editors:

Racquel Henry is a Trinidadian writer, editor, and writing coach with an MFA from Fairleigh Dickinson University. She is also a part-time English Professor and owns the writing studio, Writer's Atelier, in Maitland, FL. Racquel has been a featured author, presenter, and moderator at writing conferences and MFA residencies across the US. She is the author of the novelette, *Holiday on Park* and *The Writer's Atelier Little Book of Writing Affirmations*. Her fiction, poetry, and nonfiction have appeared in various literary magazines and anthologies. When she's not working, you can find her watching Hallmark Christmas movies.

Pamela Harris lives in Greensboro, NC and spent seven years as a middle school counselor. Currently, she is an assistant professor in the Counselor Education Department at The University of North Carolina at Greensboro. When she's not molding the minds of future school counselors, she's writing contemporary YA fiction and middle grade. Some of her favorite authors are Ellen Hopkins, Courtney Summers, Roxane Gay, and Stephen King. You can also find her at the movie theaters every weekend or pretending to enjoy exercising. She received her MFA in creative writing from Fairleigh Dickinson University in 2012 and her PhD in Counselor Education at the College of William and Mary. Her debut novel, *When You Look Like Us* (HarperCollins), releases in winter 2020.

Marquita "Quita" Hockaday lives in Williamsburg, VA. She is an adjunct professor who has never been able to shake her love of writing and reading. There is always, always a book near her. Marquita is currently enjoying writing young adult (historical and contemporary)—and most recently wrote her first middle grade novel with co-editor, Pam. Some of her favorite authors are Laurie Halse Anderson, Blake Nelson, Cormac McCarthy, and Joyce Carol Oates. Marquita graduated with an MFA in creative writing from Fairleigh Dickinson University in 2012, and completed her PhD at the College of William and Mary. She is represented by Savannah Brooks.

Readers:

Donna Compton lives just outside of Washington, D.C. and graduated from the University of Maryland University College with a Bachelor's degree in Psychology. She began taking creative writing courses a few years ago, with a focus on short stories. Currently, she's reading and writing a lot of flash fiction. Her other favorite genres include literary fiction, mystery, thriller, science fiction, and fantasy.

Rita Sotolongo is a published poet and registered yoga teacher in Orlando, Florida. Over the years, she has learned to integrate her two passions in order to keep sane in a chaotic world. This led to the development of her method for self-discovery combining yoga with writing—a practice she shares in workshops intended to help people breathe and break through mental, emotional and creative blocks. Her publications include poetry in *Black Fox Literary Magazine,* *Parentheses Journal* and *Petite Hound Press,* as well as a short story in the 2017 Florida Writers Association annual collection and one in the 2018 Demonic Household Anthology. She is a wife, mother and step-mom, and when not writing or practicing yoga, she spends her time navigating the domestic arena. Learn more about Rita by visiting yogaandwriting.com.

Contents:

Fiction

Poetry

Cover Art

Lady Ablaze
By Jennifer Battisti

It happened the night after I dog-eared the glossy page
in her hardcover book: *TimeLife Mysteries of The Unknown.*
When you're a kid, you feel pretty elitist diagnosing your
parents of their afflictions, pasting labels to them— neon
sticker-dots at garage sales. I licked my smart little thumb and
bent the corner down to mark my place next to the photograph
of a pair of shoes beneath a black smudge where a person once
was. The book said, *usually overweight spinsters with alcohol
and tobacco problems.* Sometimes, my mother left her
wedding band in the soap dish. She was a thin woman, not too
flabby, but she smoked True Blue 100's, the soft pack usually
resting in the coffin of a red leather case with a lighter tucked
inside. Just after midnight, while drinking her Ernest and
Gallo box wine and folding still-warm towels from the dryer,
she burst into flames.

I was asleep when something like backdraft woke me
to find the armchair empty of my mother. A blackened outline
of her body tattooed the fabric like a shadow she'd unzipped.
The only remains were her eyeglasses, warped from heat and a
charm bracelet lying limp, like a witness, near her glass of
cheap, rosy booze. The detective called it *combustion.* He
inspected old cigarette burns, places where past cherries had

dilated and burned—had smoldered secrets into the leather chair. When the forensics team swept the ashes, my mother billowed up, a rush of her Tresor perfume stirred to life in the soot. I knew she'd be angry at the careless way we ruined the carpet with our sooty shoes, how we paid no attention to her twin finches, Frick and Frack, going apeshit in their cage at the horror they'd seen. I blamed myself. I feared telekinesis; that my questioning was an ember, my smug finger-pointing, the fire-starter. I'd grow weary of all things *spontaneous.* As an adult, I'd avoid detours on road trips, afternoon quickies, sudden storms, punchlines of any kind. I would extinguish impulse with rigidity.

After returning to the book to unfold the page a dozen times (against medical advice), I discover the word *shrew.* I say it so many times it becomes a meaningless sound my mouth can make, like a yawn I can't stomp out. I hunt a mouse-like creature I once saw as a child—that shifty-eyed rodent who zoomed over my mother while she passed out in her chair. How could I have forgotten this? His jagged flint-filled teeth. I tunnel my fingers into the burn holes in the chair, into the web of stuffing suffocating the metal coils. Is this the escape route, the place for missing mothers and shrews, the flammable relief? I bait my tongue with blushed zinfandel and wait, cocked hammer of my mouth, to snap the spring of the trap.

Selected Poems by Madeline Miele

Therapy

There, you see? I've told you what you want to know. Last week it rained at night and no one remembers. All the leaves sliced into the concrete with the dark throb of a cut that will scar someday but is too deep now to bleed. From here it seems your window carves into the trees. For many years I have watched small grains of light flake off the sill and never once wondered what you see. Don't read this allegorically. Had I wanted to write myself out of the room I would have. Sometimes a thought rubs along the inside of a thin pipe like the after-beat of wings. Where you're looking now, all glass corners and glistening, I lean against, then ask you to repeat. I remember in childhood the glint of a pond in the woods. I felt, kneeling by the edge, I could reach down and rake the thick mud. That there may be a smooth bottom no one had ever broken the soft boat of their body to see. I'm using language here to complicate what I mean. Perhaps what you've wanted all along is to help me understand a moment the way I understand those perfect stenciled leaves and half-wet concrete.

Night Swim
for Flora

They take the day as it is given,
cinched like the tight-tipped
blossom of a fruit-bearing tree.
Sometimes a storm without warning.
Then mirrors. Tossed light
touching an empty space.
Each night it is this slow
split of the spine. A tear
in the tissue where age begins.
And the truth of a small shadow
in the half dark as they glide
through bruised water
knowing their season.
The way we know a glass
by what fills it.

.

Selected Poems by Seth Jani

Before The Storm

When the rain comes
the smeared footsteps of pollen
are washed away like ancient roads.
A small voice insinuates itself
into the space between houses,
into the paused breaths of lovers
idling on the grass.
We walk as though hushed
by a single finger,
a long, white knuckle of the wind.
Come softly, it says, as we enter
the maelstrom,
as we step into the darkening fold.

Night Train

The moon is as close
as we get to the truth.
Its secondhand light is better
than a theory of shadows,
better than bodies felt
in darkness, guessed at,
named from our misconceptions,
the mistaken shapes of things.
It's not quite Plato's Cave
but the valley fills
with luminescence.
In the distance,
a train pulls its sputtering torsos.
Its light is also borrowed.
Our pane-pressed faces
halo into sleep.

Clinging to Coral Reef
By Ollie McLean

Basil, Imogene's Irish twin, splashed in the shallows while she waited for him, cross-legged and in her nightgown, just beyond the wet lip of the ocean. He was eleven months older than her, and their mother had once told them that makes them twins. *Irish* twins. Imogene had just celebrated her thirteenth birthday and the two of them were in that sweet spot of the year where they were the same age. Usually, Imogene relished in the twenty-three days she had to brag and rub it in his face, especially since he gloated for the other eleven months of the year, but this year she didn't care as much. She was thirteen. She was something special.

"'Gene come swim with me! It's like bathwater in here!" Basil shouted. Imogene shook her head and rested her chin on her knees.

"Oh, don't be such a baby, get in!"

"I don't even have my suit on," she called back, gesturing to the cotton nightgown.

"Who cares? Just go in your unders," he said. He stomped out of the water and stood between her and the blaring sun. The skin across his chest stretched to nearly translucent, and a peppering of acne had begun to crawl across his neck.

"I don't want anybody to see me, Basil. I'm getting too old for all that." Her own nakedness had recently begun to perturb her. Since her birthday, it felt like she awoke every day to find another body part had grown longer in the night: an arm, a leg, her neck. She felt as though soon her arms would droop to the ground and her legs would drag behind and she would have to roll herself along like a coughed-up hairball just to get around. At night, in the safety of her overstuffed comforter and under the watchful eye of her teddy bear Flopsy, she would tuck her arms into her nightgown to keep them from spilling over her bed and into the hallway.

"Whatever! You think you're grown or something all of a sudden because you're *thirteen?* You know my birthday is in five days, right?" He shivered, lips beginning to blue and he clutched the waistband of a shredded pair of basketball shorts to keep them from sliding down his gaunt frame. Imogene made a mental note to take the rock-hard mint chocolate chip ice cream out of the deep freezer when she got home to let it thaw in time for dessert after dinner.

"Fine, but let's go around to the big pool," she said, "and we got to hurry to get back home because *you know* Momma's going to need help fixing dinner." Imogene had not intended for this comment to come out with the sharpened edge that it had, but it did, and she watched her brother carefully. He was defensive of their mother, and Imogene was tired from not sleeping well; she had no energy to bicker. But Basil didn't respond, rather took off in a sprint down the beach, all legs and elbows and unabashed energy.

--

The big pool was a large horseshoe tide pool where the ocean and intercoastal came together in one kiss of sand. It had been created by the tyrannical Hurricane Matthew the previous fall. In the damp days after the storm, the residents of Edisto Beach had come together to clear the debris that littered the streets, parks, and beaches. Groups of men piled truck beds with palm fronds, dock planks, patio furniture, anything that the storm had been able to pry free and skip across the asphalt.

One rather memorable afternoon was spent digging out a shiny Harley Davidson from a sandy grave on the beach, the men crouched around the bike while making delicate swipes with hand brushes like archeologists. Load after load of trash went to the dump until the downtown streets were mostly clear again and the beach resembled a beach, albeit one bent and scooped and cratered by the storm.

Imogene and Basil had done their part in the cleanup—they walked the beach scouting lightweight trash like plastic planters and tangles of fishing line. Each night for a week, Imogene came home exhausted but slept deep and sound and dreamt of blowing breezes. Unlike her mother, Imogene loved to clean. She loved the fresh inhale that came after working for an hour to unwind rotten rope choking a sago palm, leaving behind nothing but sand and a happy plant. In an act that reminded Imogene very much of their mother, Basil came home every night during the week of the cleanup with his pockets full of dirty trinkets: the bottom half of a child's toy, fishing lures, broken ceramic. He gave them to their mother who would find the handful of trash a special place in a house already overflowing with too much stuff.

--

"Imogene, hurry the hell up wouldya, and come look at this!" Basil shouted to her as she approached the edge of the tide pool. The tide was nearly all the way out, so the water level in the pool was low and out of sight from the surrounding beach. When she reached the edge, Basil was bent double over the water's surface, one arm on the slope of the dune propping him into a boney tripod. Beneath him, the water roiled; something dark, and gray, and sandy.

"What is that?" Imogene asked, but thought she recognized the pointed fin. She brought a hand to her mouth.

"It's a shark, dummy," said Basil.

A mound of sand fully covered one of the shark's pectoral fins and anchored it to the wall of the tide pool. The receding water lapped at its tail and side, but white patches of salt had left rings across its back and head. A deep red winked at them from the accordion slits that were the opening and closing of gills. It thrashed against the buried fin.

"What's it doing in here, you think? I didn't think there were sharks in the tide pool," Basil said. Imogene rolled her eyes. Sometimes she felt like they were living on different planets.

"Of course there are sharks in here, it's the *ocean*," she said. "It looks like he got stuck, though, poor little guy. Take him out of there and put him back in the deep water."

"Yeah, poor guy," Basil said, yanking the shark free. He shuffled backward into thigh-high water and dipped it under the surface. It twitched its tail and contorted in Basil's arms.

"Feel it, Imogene," he said, "come feel it, it's so rough. It's like rougher than sandpaper. Rougher than anything you've ever felt." He grinned up at her where she was still standing on the lip of the tide pool. "Unless of course you're scared."

"I'm not scared of a stupid baby shark, but I told you I don't want to get in the water, and now I *really* don't want to get in. Plus, the tide is like all the way out. Take him out to the ocean. I'm just going to go home, okay? Meet me there."

"Wait, 'Gene, what if we could keep it?" Basil said as Imogene turned around to walk away.

"Keep what? Keep a shark?" She huffed a laugh of pure mocking then regretted it when she saw a flicker of pain behind Basil's eyes. "Where would you put it?"

He shrugged and cooed and pet the shark under the water. "I don't know, you think Mom would let me put it in the bathtub just for like a night or something?" Again, Imogene wondered how they could be living in such different realities. She and her mother would make the occasional private joke about Basil—he could get from A to B, but he had to make a detour at XYZ first.

"No, I don't, plus her bathtub has all that scrapbooking crap in it," she said, holding in a sigh.

"There's got to be somewhere we could keep it," he said.

Imogene's patience was running on a familiar empty tank. "You *could* just take the stupid thing out to the ocean and let it go! You don't *need* a shark and you can't take care of a shark! Get rid of it!" She shouted at him and turned around to walk home. "Don't be late for dinner, either!"

When Imogene opened the door, she knew instantly her mother had burned the garlic bread Imogene had chosen for dinner. Shrugging her beach bag off her shoulder, she scanned the living room for a bag of chips. Recently their home had become messier than she remembered. The shopping bags of unopened toys and random home décor that usually resided in the margins of the living room had slowly crept onto the couch and into the center of the floor, like an ever-rising tide, leaving only a small patch of the carpet underneath exposed in the center of the floor. Towers of neglected newspapers and fashion catalogs slipped coupon innards onto the floor where her family was forced to walk on them and leave behind crushed clip outs in the shape of their footprints as clear evidence of their comings and goings. The tracks perturbed Imogene. She couldn't go to the bathroom without leaving behind a perfect trail for anyone to follow and track her down.

What used to be their dining room was stacked knee-and-head high with books, cardboard and plastic boxes, puffs of clothing here and there. To get to the vine-choked backyard, Imogene had to pick her way along paths she had carved in the toppling cavern walls of stuff like an animal digging itself from the ruins of a burned forest. Opening the sliding-glass door meant rearranging the balance of sheets and water bottles and an insufferable amount of unboxed toys that her mother had stacked against it.

--

Her mother lived for shopping. When Imogene and Basil had been small children, she would take them on day-long shopping trips that she called "runs." Imogene's favorite run was the day after Halloween when they went to the Halloween Outlet and their mother let them pick out anything they wanted. Imogene covered her hair with plastic spider clips, Basil became a rotation of horrifying masks, and their mother filled five shopping carts and burned through three credit cards.

Back at home, the van vomited bite-size Snickers and campy lawn decorations onto the driveway. The three of them sat on the carpet in the living room for hours afterward looking through the treasure. Their mother still lived for shopping, but she did most of it from catalogs and QVC now.

"Imogene, is that you? Can you come help me for a second, baby?" her mother called.

In the kitchen, her mother stood at the open space where the stovetop steamed among towers of Tupperware containers and unopened packages of paper towels. She turned from a pot on the stove, flashed a smile at Imogene, and extended one bangled arm for a hug.

"How was the beach, my love?" she said into Imogene's hair. She smelled like cucumber melon body spray and the cakey makeup she bought from television ads.

Imogene shrugged. "It was good. Basil found a shark and was being stupid about it," she said.

"'Gene, be nice," her mother said, releasing her. "Besides, I thought you liked sharks and animals and all that." She waved a hand in the air as she stirred tomato sauce on the stove. After a few seconds, she turned again and looked Imogene up and down. "Did you wear your nightgown to the beach?"

"Yeah, I couldn't find my bathing suit," she said and looked down.

"Oh come on, I just bought you at least three suits this year! What about that great pink one with the little tassels? That would look so pretty against your pale skin!"

"I don't know, Momma, I just couldn't find it okay? There's just too much shit in there."

"Imogene! You watch your mouth!" She turned and shot Imogene a glare that told her she had gone too far but that she wasn't in real trouble.

"Grab me a pack of noodles," she said, "they're under the big box of diapers over there." Imogene dug under the pile.

"How did you know that?" she asked, handing her the box. Her mother laughed her *hee-haw* laugh that made Imogene wince.

"I just remember."

--

Last year, Imogene had cleaned the floor of her room by sorting through everything and putting every item on trial for its life. She threw away every scrap of trash and anything dirty or stained in a big black garbage bag. When she could finally sit on the floor, she brought her mother to see. At the threshold of her room, her mother pressed a hand to her mouth and gripped the doorframe a little too hard, her neon pink nails catching the wood.

"You did this?" she asked, tears in her eyes.

"It's nice, right, Momma?" Imogene had said.

"Yes, baby, I'm so proud of you. Did you throw a lot away?"

"Just some old stuff."

"Old stuff like what?"

"Just some old magazines and some really dirty things, but it was all trash. It feels nice in my room now. I'm going to keep it like this forever."

That night their mother brought in the big black garbage bag from outside and sorted through everything

Imogene had put in it. She then told Imogene not to throw anything else away without talking to her first.

"What do you want all those dirty magazines for?" Imogene had asked her. Her mother looked up at the ceiling and ran a filthy hand through her hair.

"I don't know, baby. It's like when I throw it away, I lose the memory of looking at it. Like I lose that whole day."

--

Basil arrived home from the beach just as a fresh batch of garlic bread was coming out of the oven. He slammed the front door, as usual, and walked to the kitchen to get a soda from the refrigerator. Imogene was digging the ice cream from its frozen grave in the deep freezer when he came up behind her and whispered in her ear.

"I left it in the tide pool so I could go back and see it later."

Imogene pushed the ice cream into his chest and said, "Well, that was stupid. The tide is going to go all the way out, and it's going to die."

"No way, I'm definitely going to be back in time, and then I'll just move it to deeper water. I can keep doing that and feed it and stuff and before you know it, I'm going to have a pet freaking *shark* and you're going to be so freaking jealous."

Basil wolfed down his bowl of spaghetti, sending flecks of tomato sauce into the air as though he were washing his face in it. The three of them sat side by side on the couch, the only available seats in the house, and watched an episode of *Bevis and Butthead*, eating from Styrofoam bowls on their laps. Their mother talked through all the music videos and scoffed at what she called "toilet humor."

Right before he dashed out to go back to the beach, Basil emptied his pockets into their mother's outstretched hands. There were two crumpled flowers and a piece of shell so covered in algae that it had little dark green mouths all over it. Their mother clucked, kissed her hands, and danced down the goat path to the kitchen sink window where she placed the flowers and shell on top of the decayed remains of other days' flowers and shells; a gray and ghoulish menagerie.

Imogene watched Basil leave and wondered about the little shark trapped in the drying tide pool. She felt a pang of guilt and something like the ever-increasing weight of responsibility, but the expanse of her bed was calling to her.

--

Imogene had to make constant attempts to keep the tsunami of stuff from breaking down the door to her room. For most of her childhood, she dealt with sharing her room with her mother's shopping habit. She reconciled with herself: it would be silly for her to be upset that her mother enjoyed buying her new clothes and toys. Then she got older and started expanding—it was like she didn't stop where her body stopped, like her skin was no indication of where *she* ended—and she needed more space. She was suffocating under piles of tutus and pallets of soda and two-size-too-small denim blazers with the tags on them.

And hiding stuff in clutter is not as easy as it may seem, especially with a mother as perceptive as Imogene's. Her mother would come home from a day-long shopping run, bags stiff with overpriced makeup brushes, faux fur muffs, gilded jewelry boxes, brass cutlery, and she would stand in the middle of the living room, in the single shrinking patch of carpet, red rings on her arms where the heavy bags had been biting her on the walk from the car, and huff and puff, her eyes welling up and a panic pulling at the corners of her mouth, until Imogene would finally give in and let her shove *just a couple* bags in the corner of her closet.

Then in the night, Imogene would sneak out into the house to find pockets where she could hide one t-shirt or a single mascara tube until the bags were empty and the free space in the house had only shrunk to the well-trained eye and she had reclaimed some of her precious square footage. Occasionally her mother would notice a rogue Christmas ornament that had been in Imogene's room and say something in a sing-song voice about it. This often came shortly before she would show up with more stuff to store.

--

Imogene closed the door to her room and fell face first onto her bed. The momentary quiet of a soft bedspread had a calming effect on her. At least there was no junk on her bed, and she was going to *keep it that way.* She leaned over the edge and plugged in a string of Christmas lights she had stapled across the wall above her then grabbed her copy of the latest installment of the *Goosebumps* series. It was titled *My Best Friend is Invisible.* On the cover, a cat is terrorized by a floating pizza box and can of soda. Imogene sympathized with the cat.

Her mother cracked the door open and tapped a knock, something she had started doing lately and it drove Imogene nuts. Smiling sheepishly, she said, "Can I come in a minute?"

Imogene tucked her legs under her to make room for her mother to sit down. She had noticed that if she was quiet for stretches of time, people would get bored or confused and leave her alone, so she tried to stay still and wait for her mom to speak or, preferably, to leave.

"It seemed like a really nice day to go to the beach," her mom said. Imogene nodded. After a few beats, her mother looked at her and said, "I spoke to Tyger today."

Tyger was Imogene's mother's off-and-on prison inmate boyfriend. They had met during a Christmas Mission Drive at the prison two years before. Her mother had overseen collecting donations and taking them to the church; and Tyger, a low-security inmate with privileges, was responsible for organizing the inventory for the prison. They had spent an hour one evening sharing a thermos of coffee and counting boxes of socks as they were unloaded from the back of her minivan and sorted into sizes.

In the weeks following, there were letters that had evolved into phone calls, until eventually, Imogene's mother was driving the hour journey three times a week to visit Tyger at the prison. It all stopped one day in a fit of collect calls and tears and shouting and her mother's shopping habits skyrocketed and the patch of carpet in the living room shrunk smaller and smaller. But it wasn't *over* over, of course, it had all started up again, and then ended again. Up and down. Smaller and smaller.

But now, Imogene was expanding out of her body faster than she could hide things around the house, and Basil was trying to keep a shark in the bathtub, and all she wanted was to sleep, but she was being haunted by a floating pizza box and a can of soda and her mother was speaking to Tyger *again*.

Stay cool. Be still, and quiet—she might go away.

"He told me to tell you hi," she said.

Imogene scoffed. She hadn't *really* meant to do it. The sound exploded out of her like one of those mushrooms that if you stomp on it, a velvet spore cloud puffs around your foot and floats off on air. Her mom narrowed her eyes at her.

"What?" she said.

"Nothing. Tell him I said hi." Imogene knew she sounded pouty and bratty, but she didn't care.

"Okay, good," her mom used the voice that said she didn't want to have a real conversation, that she just wanted Imogene to listen and agree with her. "He's doing really well, you know, he has been taking Spanish classes and he's talking to a therapist once a week. He was asking all about you and Basil."

"Cool," Imogene said. She scratched her thumbnail down the book's spine.

"It is cool. He's a really *cool* guy," she said and paused, watching Imogene scratch at the book. "And he's also been talking to a transition therapist."

Imogene tensed at the tone in her voice. "What is that?"

"Well, baby, he's going to be getting out in a couple months, and, well I was thinking he could come live here with us."

Something moved in the corner of Imogene's room—it was a cellar spider scurrying across the floor from under her door, the tsunami leaking in one infiltrator at a time. There wasn't enough space in here for Imogene, her mother, and the spider. She was going to lose her mind.

"Why would he want to come live here?" were the words that came out. For a moment, her mother's face held taught—a rosy smile under bleached hair—then it cracked and she frowned deep.

"Gee, I don't know 'Gene, don't you think maybe 'cause we love each other? And because I love you two so much, too much, and I want you to have a daddy?"

"Mom, did you tell him he could come live here?" Heat lit up her ears and chest. The spider had crawled under her dresser. Her mother didn't say anything, and they sat there together on her bed sharing the stale, dusty air. Her mother's face was splotchy and she was biting her middle fingernail.

"It's not *that* bad in here," her mom said. "It won't take that long to clean up. It could be a fun project! I bet Basil will be excited to help."

Imogene's head wobbled on her impossibly long neck. Her arms were loose in the sockets of her shoulders and her breath rushed in and out of her open throat.

"It's horrible here! All this shit that nobody wants. We need to clean this shit up!" Imogene threw her book to the side of her bed and it slid off in a more dramatic gesture than she had intended.

"Imogene! Your language! We will—I will clean it up! And anyways, I was thinking—what if we moved? Huh? What if we moved into a bigger house? I saw a few really nice houses for sale on Belcher."

Imogene needed to get out of the stiff atmosphere of her house. Her mother's bright face was blinding, the naiveté palpable and crazymaking. She leapt from her bed and pulled on a pair of jeans from the floor. Bursting from the front door, the salty air outside clung to her face.

--

Out on the beach, she scanned for Basil's headlamp, spotting it bouncing in the shadows. She could see he was on his knees in the surf and as she approached, she heard him muttering to himself.

"Hey, how's the shark?" she called to him when she got close.

"I think it's dying," Basil said, his voice sticky with tears. "I'm trying to get some water through its gills." He cradled the shark and rocked it in the water. It was very still. A wave washed up and over her bare feet and she had the sudden urge to throw off her clothes and dive into the dark water. She knelt next to Basil.

"I know you told me not to leave it there. That was so stupid of me," he said.

"You didn't mean to hurt it, you know. It's okay. It didn't look too good to begin with, honestly. It's like the survival of the fittest. Some of them are just supposed to die."

"I should have listened to you and just let it go," he said. He shook it back and forth in the water, little pumping motions with his arms. "I keep seeing his gills moving and I'm thinking if I can just get enough water to them maybe he will be okay."

She leaned forward and pulled Basil's head down to shine the light of his headlamp on the shark. Quickly, without thinking much about it, she reached her fingers between the delicate flaps of skin, pinched the red meat and pulled. It was over almost instantly. Blood flowed onto the sand and the waves gathered it up then brought it into the ocean. Something in the shark's gills sliced her finger and Imogene's blood dripped down her hand and mingled in the surf where it, too, was washed away.

--

Basil held onto the body of the shark for a long time, leaning on Imogene until his sobs were sniffles. His face was swollen from crying and he was trembling. Eventually, he stood and walked down the beach, the shark's head and tail spilling from his arms. Imogene followed him all the way to the defunct fishing pier; she followed him up the sand-crusted steps and past the cleaning station, iridescent with fish scales; she followed him past the statue of Eggleston, the famous one-legged pelican; past coils of ropes waiting for someone to come uncoil them and tether one world to the other; and past fuel lines that jutted into the sky on rusted springs. He stopped at the end of the dock and clicked off his headlamp.

"It's okay," she said when she reached his side. "Are you okay?"

He nodded, and said, "Mm-hmm," then dropped the corpse of the little shark into space. It twisted in the air for a millennium before splashing into the ocean. Imogene couldn't see it in the obscured darkness, but they waited together in the wind until the wild had reclaimed it.

Selected Poems by Arjun Parikh

This Fate

A kestrel treads the blood-tinged sky,
Waiting for the world to stir.
She holds the sinking sun in one eye,
The open country in the other.

She waits in this way for hours,
Hovering, keeping trembling hearts
On a knife edge. There is always one who cowers,
Whose resolve to brave the light falls apart.

And when that one does, the kestrel will plunge
To this scorched earth, this aching soil,
Where those who know leap but never lunge,
Where those who are blessed with wings do not toil.

If you were a kestrel, you would see
A silhouette waning into darkness, waiting for you
To plunge to this fate, to plunge for me,
To give in to your heart that beats for ruin.

This Side of Pain

It takes four breaths to own a silence,
But just one to fall from love.
It takes four heartbeats to know a body,
But just one, when push comes to shove

To shuffle your feet to the edge. You look down:
The world is so elegant from above.
All is still but wings and water,
Yet this will never be enough.

You do not fall, you do not jump.
Here, there is only surrender.
You open your arms and hug the looming sea.
You pray that you may enter.

You are falling, yes, you are falling
Beside a drop of rain.
You have never known grace, not like this.
It happens on this side of pain.

forest spirits
By Jenna Dirksen

stay with me until
your lips grow green
with moss
red skin peeled raw
underneath
      all dark

Heroin: An Interview
By R. Nikolas Macioci

Where do you put the needles, I ask. Arms,
legs, stomach, hands, you answer. What
does it feel like, I ask. You get to edge
your way off the earth. You fall through
the air until things are right, you answer.
Do you understand life better when you
are high, I ask. You understand that the
whole mystery sucks. Aren't you afraid
of the danger, I ask. My drugs are very
dear to me. Everything sorts itself out
when you're high, you answer. Do you
feel lucky so far not to have died, I ask.
My life resembles a grave. I'm happy to
take the chance, you answer. Are you
ever afraid during a high, I ask. I'm safe.
I know what I'm doing, you answer. How
did your addiction begin, I ask. At fourteen,
my parents introduced me to heroin. My
father died of an overdose, you answer.
May I ask one last question: What is the
likelihood that you will ever seek help,
I ask. Never. I never want to see my life
up close again. And with that answer you
wrap a rubber tube around your forearm,
slip the tip of a silver needle into the basilica
vein.

Selected Poems by Terry Minchow-Proffitt

For the Record

For the record, I only wanted to sing songs.
                    –Kathleen Edwards

This morning in 7-11
I say, *How's it going, Derrien?*
Startled, the young clerk
catches himself and smiles,
I'm still not used to hearing my name.
Wonder how
do you know my name?
Then I remember.
He taps his black badge
with white lettering: *Derrien.*

Maybe the days hold
only time and money
spent, maybe I should mind my own business.
But I don't. I say, *And I'm Terry*
as our hands touch over change.

On other days at 7-11 I've been known
to say the names
Maggie, or *Neal,*
others who wear black badges.
But not always.

For the record, I curate.
I measure out whole octaves.
I could have said:

It's not fair, Derrien, to be forced
to be nailed by your name
for minimum wage, to pretend
intimacy, to be exposed for so little.
But you're here and I,
glad to say your name, grateful
to share my own, think,
how rare, how big already
this day.

But the line was long
and I could not hold that note.

Maybe It Was Monday

Mr. Boyce would come home
early in the summer after pulling
the graveyard shift at Mohawk,
rush breakfast and put off sleep
to hit flies. For you and his sons
he'd do that. In his sleeveless t-shirt
and worker's khakis he could
knock them high and easy and
take in with red-rimmed eyes
how we ran underneath to size up
each fly ball till one of us
called *Mine*! Each catch
a little heaven
held for a moment
in the glove,
in the day's first light,
then thrown back
like it was nothing.
Maybe it was Monday

like this morning, still
echoing the heave and haste
of last Monday, shadowing well
into the cusp of this new day
until morning lights
bareback on a highline wire
and you watch it ride off west.

Seven days equals a week,
and lots of those mean years.
That's an equation
that's never proven to hold me—
not like the provident morning light
and those who rise to meet it
in the world we belong to,
how it lands now
as something in the eyes,
and catches *Mine!* in the throat.

Thank-You Notes

In his last years, he slowed down
enough to take a shine
to thank-you notes. He was one
of those people. Sometimes sent
out six at a time. The impulse
to own brief
exhalations of debt
by pen, on paper,
folded and slipped
into more paper. Licked
and sealed. Sweet gum
and trees on the tongue.

No two-bit binary wisps

that warrant the metallic jut and edge
of cell towers, but the pliant,
some small thing taken on
clumsily, hand-written, hand-delivered
That you'd make the time means the world
to where you live, a thin leaf
that must be picked
up and torn open,
then read.

You remember reading?
How the left-handed cursive
scrawls along and tilts down
and away, the downstream
sway of driftwood?
Every sent note shouldered
by a million and one unsent.
Thanks like held breath,
roiling, rising irrepressible.

The Pinball Machine
By Lawrence Cady

I watch him just now. He's thinking about something.
A friend at school, maybe a teacher, maybe his pseudo-
girlfriend, Faith. He's content, though. Pleased about whatever
it is he's thinking, and as always happens when he's like this I
can't help but watch him out the corner of my eye and think,
All's good. All's as it should be.

Los Angeles and the urban sprawl it is comes into view
as our gondola rounds the very top of the great circle Pacific
Park's Ferris wheel completes maybe one hundred times a
day. LA, the Ferris wheel, neither is important; *he* is a marvel,
a twelve-year-old one of a kind.

It is, I'm thinking once again, just another day at
Pacific Park. Just another day. We've been here so many times
it might as well be our backyard instead of the down-sloped,
rocky hillside that is our backyard behind our—I should say
my wife *Isabel's*—pretentious mini mansion in Laurel
Canyon. That place neither Liam nor I care a whole hell of a
lot for, but that's okay, that's fine. We've got Pacific Park,
Paradise Cove, Newport Beach. We've got our little world of
contentment all carved out, and I couldn't be more pleased
with it.

"Hey, Dad," Liam says, seeing that I'm watching him but, cool customer he is, making no mention of it. "Let's go. Enough rides for now."

"Ready to go home?"

"No, not yet. Let's just hang at the pier. Just a little longer."

The great wheel decelerates, our gondola gliding downward and straight into place at the bottom of the circle that is the loading platform. The ride attendant, a weather-worn, gray-bearded man in a crimson turban, who reminds me of a Pacific Park regular I once knew, though he's much too old to be one and the same, swings the gondola door open and says, "All right now, rides over." His accent is distinctly Punjabi.

We go down the creaking platform steps and follow the natural flow of the crowd toward the pier proper, where we angle seaward, the very end of the pier, we both know, our final destination. This has been a ritual for us all along. We spend time at the beach, maybe dip into the ocean waves if it's warm, and head straight for Pacific Park and ride the rides. An hour or two later, a little spent, a little too much of a good thing, and we take a minute out on the pier. For Liam, it's the *coming down* off a kid-fun high, and he switches gears and is ready for some downtime and then the trip home, where he'll do some homework, watch some TV, get on the computer. For me, our time together at the end of the day is nine-tenths of what I'm here for. A kid who's had his fun, his adventure, is a kid who, more times than not, opens up, lets you in without your having to ask: *Things cool at school, Liam? Teachers okay? What's up with Faith? How's she?*

And lucky for me, he seems ready to talk on this day, though thinking about it I'm not sure what day it is.

We take a bench that faces due west, the Pacific a vast, secretive water world we can only contemplate from afar. Funny thing, we're alone all of a sudden. Though it's mid-afternoon—this is usually the busiest time of day, especially out here—it seems we're amazingly alone.

"Hell, Liam," I say, glancing behind us and seeing that, except for a small girl and her dog, the pier is all but vacated. "Where'd everybody go? It's like someone's called in a bomb threat."

"I know," Liam says, his eyes fixed on the distant horizon. "It's crazy, huh?"

"I mean, the rides were packed full, the lines were ridiculous, and now this?" I stand, looking all around, and the little girl that was there just a minute ago is gone too.

"Well, Dad, it's just like that now. It's just us here, really."

"I guess. Well let's take a minute, but then we go. I'm a little spooked here. Something's up with no one here."

"Dad, you've forgotten something, though."

"What's that?"

"It's 2018, Dad. You're tricked because of what's happened."

"What's happened?"

"Someone shot you. Like with a gun. *Shithead*, I think you call him. Drug dealer type. But that doesn't matter. I'm just glad to see you, Dad." He offers up a hug, arms around my neck and shoulders. I hear a kind of strained whimper emanate from within him. "I've missed you a lot, Dad. A real lot."

"Me too," I say, my voice catching in my throat. "I'm sorry for everything. Every-goddamn-thing. I'm sorry."

"Nothing to be sorry about, Dad. Nothing."

He smiles now. He's himself, age twelve.

"*Shit happens*, right Dad? We always used to say that."

"I remember." I glance back once again in the direction of the beach, where a lone elderly woman in a tan pantsuit is coming our way. "You always knew when to swear, Liam, and when not to. You were smart that way, kind of cool."

"Thanks."

"You know, you're just as I remember you, Liam," I say, the notion that this is 2018 beginning to register. "You're twelve. But if what you said is true, you'd be in your twenties by now."

"I'm twelve, Dad. I'm twelve."

"Well I'm not making much sense of any of this, but I'm not sure I give a shit."

"You shouldn't give a shit. Not today."

Another hug, pats on the backs, no words said.

"Jesus, Liam, The Scrambler. Just about killed me," I say, if anything to break our silence. "It messed me up *again*!"

Liam laughs, his beaming face all smiles and a little taunting. "You never liked The Scrambler. Never. I always knew that, from the first time we went on it. I was in, like, second grade I think. Every time you'd get off it the first thing you'd do is shake your hands and your feet like you're shaking off getting hit by a linebacker."

We both laugh, Liam beside himself, and though I'm ecstatic, back where I fucking belong for the first time in a long time, I sense that within I'm on the verge of breaking down, falling to the pier planking in a heap, a decade's worth of tears striking me all at once.

"Your laugh," I say, shaking my head. "I've missed that like you wouldn't know. I can't tell you, Liam. I can't put it into words. It's like—"

"It's like you lost your best goddamn friend," Liam says, looking down at his torn Chuck Taylors. "I know, Dad. It's like that for me too. We can't help that, but it's not forever, you know. You couldn't have known that, though, and I'm sorry for that. I'm sorry you had to feel so bleak, so out of it. That hurt me more than ending up dead. Seriously."

"You know, Liam, the things you're saying. If anyone were here to hear us they'd think we're crazy."

He laughs, his happy-kid face a delight.

"That you're here at all, Liam, that you're still twelve and it's already 2018, I don't get it. What's happened here?"

"This is one of those places I go sometimes. It's a place that's just mine. I made it up and it's my own place."

"Your own place where? In an afterlife? You're saying this is your afterlife?"

"Well, not really. There is no afterlife. There's something else, though. It's a kind of *conjuration*, I've heard some say, but I'm new at it. I'm just beginning to figure it out. No one figures it out completely until, like, they're old. Really, really old."

"Where'd you go, Liam? You and your mother? After Paris, I mean. After the car wreck. You went here?"

"Sort of."

"Where's she?"

"I don't know."

"Are you happy here or wherever it is? Are you cool?"

"Most of the time, yeah. Very cool. I have these friends. All kinds of friends. In death, Dad—and by the way, you're goddamn lucky to be hearing this. Really lucky. I wish I'd have heard it instead of having to find it out. But in death, you go flying off, like through these skyways or arteries or something, to all these different places that aren't like what Earth is. It's more like this giant pinball machine. I mean, one that's so big, so voluminous, you have to map it out and figure it out as you go. That's kind of what you do. You find your way in this crazy pinball machine by mapping things out."

"No God, just a pinball machine."

"No God, at least I think not. Some would argue that, but not me. But what you do is move through different places, lots of them, too many to count, and you stay in each place for a while and you acquire friends and you learn things, like how to alter your path through the machine so you can go to other places you think you would like and avoid places you think you wouldn't like. It's not exactly that, the way I'm saying it, but sort of. You meet others, some you like, some you don't like. But it's all fair. It's a fair game and you don't really lose. Like just now, today, I didn't know I was coming here, and I didn't know for sure I'd see you right now, though I sensed that I would. I was in a place that had mostly trees and mountains, and I was with some friends and it was nice, but I kind of bounced out of it without my knowing that was going to happen. That's why I call it a pinball machine. You're somewhere one minute, but then you're bounced out to somewhere else and you're there for a time. Who runs the machine, the game? No one seems to know. There are theories, but really it's not anything anyone knows too much about."

"Do you see your mother?"

"Sometimes I do. Here and there. She was sad, I mean when we first entered into the machine together after the accident. She was scared like I was and I think everyone is at first. But you get over that pretty quick. You have to."

"Will I see you again? I mean, another time?"

"Sure you will. But you'll probably have to be dead first. You'll have to leave all that, which, I've learned, is only a special case of what everything is, which is the pinball machine."

"You're not trapped, are you? Inside this machine?"

"No, not at all. It's the opposite of that. It's not a machine really, it's places that are all interconnected. Different ways of living. We're not, like, human anymore, but we still are, too."

I can't help but look at him with extreme, put-on doubt, my eyes set big and questioning the way I used to when he was a little kid and pulling my leg. He laughs uproariously now at my exaggerated face, which he must have seen a thousand times when he was a toddler.

I grip his big smiling kid head with my hands and give him a sure, smacking kiss on the forehead. For all I know this dream, this visit to the so-called pinball machine, will be over any minute and he'll be gone again.

We sit for a time looking out over the Pacific, and though I have a million questions to ask, I keep my mouth shut. It's me and Liam, right here on this bench at the pier, and if I were to expire this very second, I'd be fine. I'd die knowing that I came full circle with my son and very likely I'd enter into the pinball machine with him.

Liam says, looking anywhere but at me, "Hey, Dad?"

"What's that?"

"The drugs you're always taking now. You're gonna get rid of that, right?"

"Yeah. Yeah, I'll do that. If anything on your say-so. That's impetus enough for me."

"Cool. Kill that off, okay?"

"Absolutely. For sure. But you know what I wish, Liam? I mean right now?"

"What's that?"

"I wish we could walk back down the pier like we used to, crowds or no crowds, and get in the car and head home. And I wish your mom would be there waiting for us in one of those frilly robe-gown things she used to wear. I'd give anything to go back there and do things differently. Take Paris the hell off the itinerary and do everything we were supposed to do."

"I have to say, Dad, I've thought that myself over the years, but then that wasn't what was going to happen. You know what, though, Dad?"

"What?"

"This place." He stands, his little arms wide out at his sides to indicate the width and breadth of the California coastline. "I set this all up, this place, because I knew you were coming here on a fluke. I sensed it, like I said, and I sensed you getting shot like you were, and that's how I came bouncing out here and you and I got the chance to be here at the same time. I mean, in this little slice of time. This is for you, Dad. I thought of making it the Santa Cruz Beach Boardwalk. It's like a Northern California version of Pacific Park, except it's bigger, much bigger, but it seemed the real Pacific Park was the better choice, at least for us, for now. But I set it up like this for you, for you and me. It's the only thing I could think to do."

"I'm utterly blown away, Liam. Blown away."

He smiles and it's as if he's six again.

"Coolest dad," Liam says, beaming again. "I said that a few times, didn't I? I think I did anyway."

"You did. You sure as hell did."

"Remember this day, Dad."

"I'll remember," I say and as if the pinball machine has come to claim him he offers up a five-finger wave but then dissipates like so much water vapor into the sun-streaked air. And he's gone, not a trace of him to be seen. It's just me and the bench and the pier.

I stand and watch and wait for a time, and it seems the evacuation call has come to an end, the hordes taking the pier once again. Fathers and sons, mothers and daughters, grandparents and grandkids; all here to see the sights, the sun, the sea.

With Liam having made his departure, I have no idea what to do, and so I walk aimlessly through the crowd and I'm on my own again out on the Santa Monica pier—nothing new for me. I'm pleased, though, beyond my wildest dreams to have seen him, pleased to have been visited by him. And I wonder, *Might Isabel be here? Might she have come to see Liam, maybe to see me?* It seems I owe her some sort of apology, Liam alive and well and manufacturing the entire Southern California coastline almost on a whim.

I move through the crowds hoping to catch a glimpse of her, hoping *she's* alive and well and as pleased as Liam seems to be within the confines of this pinball machine world I know nothing about.

Selected Poems by Jen Drake

Turnout
  for Po

The medicine did its work

                                    so quickly

The flesh and bone in which
I had known   and loved you   so long

            dropped

For a moment
    like the silence after singing

                you stood

        I could almost see you

And then you were away across the hill
    heart of wind

feet
        among the stars

Origin

Stirring
movement in the deeper channels
    of the brain
down there
           where the current is swift

Huge fish glittering
          moonlit silver
in cold black water

    the universe in his eye
    the globe of the world in his mouth
    & his gills
        trailing
            fire

He makes his bed
    among the roots of consciousness
    & dreams many strange creatures
          into being.

Selected Poems by Jeannine Hall Gailey

During the Month of Tornadoes, The Fox-Wife Appears (A Haibun)

The fox-wife returns
to me in a dream during
the month of tornadoes.

"I was born to disappear," she says. In a field of poppies, a fox kit approaches me, so close I can feel its breath. We both lie down to sleep. Red fur and red petals swirl, fitful, around us. The fox's smile is ever-present. My teeth are sharp as the fox's. I find myself carving my name into the ground. The name is the name of the fox who disappears like smoke. The sky is an eerie blue-green, the green is the coming storm. March delivers on its promise.

My Fox Boyfriend

Arrives every seven years, like clock-work. The first time I was seven, he was a red fox kit in a glade, in mist, standing so close I could see his breath. The second time was behind my house, he raised his tail in greeting, standing still as a statue. My fox boyfriend always leaves gifts. Sometimes a sudden-blooming stand of daffodils, or a pile of red maple leaves. Once he came to me on an island and took my picnic food. Sometimes he scares off rabbits from my yard. Now I am older, I cannot dance with him like I used to. He is quiet too, waiting for me at the edge of the forest, his face burned into my heart, a flame kiss.

The Luck of Foxes

The black fox with white-tipped tail
is good luck, while the red fox
is a trickster. Red, white, and black foxes together –
a bad omen. The gold eyes of the red fox
hold the sun in them. The black fox's fur
sometimes fades to silver, sometimes not.

The fox is here to tell you: you can survive
on beetles and river water.
The fox's lair holds two kits,
who touch muzzles with bared teeth,
a sort of affectionate threat.

Whatever the vixen brings home in her jaws
will be dinner. Three foxes together.
The fox has nothing to fear except you.
You have nothing to fear except your future, your luck,
the fate that you and fox together are weaving.

Winged Heart
By Bree Devones Hsieh

A wooden heart bought years ago
spreads hinged-open wings—

it hangs like a lesson, over my sink—
perhaps it's wondering
when I might learn how to fly,

over the range of mountains
or just beyond the fence.

So I ask when it might grow
into a creature as large as a house,
so I can climb on its back

and glance at my plot from the sky,
and it can see the trees
from which its wings were hewn.

Selected Poems by Diana Conces

Uncontrolled Powered Flight

Pine trees stretch up,
greening the winter sun,
the dog pulls ahead,
knowing the path down
to the gently foaming creek.
We run away from ourselves,
paw and dirty tennis shoes
crunching the dead pine needles.

In Florida, nine astronauts
pulled away from this life,
followed a planned trajectory
that ended in fireworks,
torpedoed into the ocean
while fragments of descent
littered an East Texas field.

There is only so far you can run
before the o-rings break,
before that mass of unburnt fuel
ignites, exploding you back
onto the unyielding ground.

Wasps

at midnight
   in the waning of the moon,
I pulled on heavy jeans,
     woolen socks, black gloves,
     heavy black trench coat,
     and, veiled like a widow,
     I strode into the garden.
A murderer, I took aim,
     methodical, pitiless,
     controlled bursts of poison
     precisely aimed,
     each nest splattered
     until dripping.
Then I faded into the night,
     Death gliding
     across the paving stones,
     the angry buzzing
     of the already dying
     left behind
     with the already dead.
I will come at dawn,
     bearing a sharp hoe
     to destroy their ruined homes
     so that at the dark of the moon
     I can light a fire
     in the chiminea
     and burn some diaries and old poems,
     the empty nests
     of my memories of you
     that stand empty and poisoned,
     pathetic in the light.

Somewhere

somewhere
in a rusted metal lockbox
buried and guarded
under sand, sealed in concrete

somewhere
in this empty landscape
the odd warning spire of cactus
amidst a jumble of broken rocks

somewhere
I made a map once
but only shaded in primary colors
no fine lines, no subtleties—so I search

somewhere
lie the meanings of your words
all their hues resplendent
waiting to be strung on the barest strand of sentence.

Inside a Gas-Lit House
By Lisa Guadio

His big brown eyes
with dilated pupils
stare at you through
round glass,
love-framed
with coffee spoons
In the sink, &
Clothes spread
across the floor; it's
milk-white & heavy-cream,
citrus beaded body wash
& warm cotton towels,
Stale pizza crust and sex games
With wine-stained teeth:

His fingers through your hair,
hands cupped over yours;
he crunches your fingers into a ball,
puts it to your chest.
He tells you the human heart is
relatively
the size
of a fist.

You try to imagine his heart,
ventricles bulging
like white knuckles
pulsing like veins
choking the bone
underneath their thick skin
His wet lips kiss your forehead
While you pretend to sleep
his drunken rage & apology the morning after

His careless stumble back inside at 2 AM
Is the burning cold ice pack.
He presses to your eye
And asks how you hurt yourself?

He cradles you like a baby
because you just had a panic attack
and as you press your ear
to his chest
you can hear his fist
beating away
against the bars of his rib cage
thumping the bones bruised
and you are happy
they are there to
protect you.

A hangover lingers
until you soak it in grease
& sleep; last night's argument sags
heavy, like a rain cloud
Until you strangle it
with eggshell apology
for causing it.

Look in the mirror.
See the red rings around your neck.
His fist above your head,
        What he said
                About the heart...

                                Does he have one?

Of course he does—
A fist is a heart.
A heart means love.
A heart beats like

A fist like
love does.

As gaslight creeps through the blinds it is in his house, not
yours. He's given you the closet and told you it's a room.
He's fed you moldy fruit and told you it was wine. He's
tucked you into bed and pressed your eyelids shut, boarded the
windows and told you they were cracked,

and as you listen to the rain along the roof, thunderclap in the
distance, he assures you there is no storm. He's created a
hurricane around you & called it a leaky faucet.

You wonder why he's never lonely & you always are. And
why you're always bleeding & he's always calling you
paranoid.

His threats have only sounded like "I love you's" so long as
you've had your ear to his chest.

But you know
there is no love;
no, you know he has no heart—
just a fist,
shaped like one.

The Mindful Act of Forgetting
By Emily Larkin

This is how you survive: carefully box your memories, and seal them away in the dustiest corner of your mind.

Images of the numerous scars on his hands.

His face, bathed in moonlight: young, hopeful and afraid.

Realizing he's showing off. Liking it.

Driving through the city at nightfall; seeing the building lights like stars thrown to earth.

Nuzzling against his shoulder.

Sharing an ice-cream while you plot the perfect crime. A cold strawberry dab on your nose. He tastes like chocolate.

Don't let a single memory escape. Search for them all and lay them in, one on top of the other. Fold them to make them fit. Squeeze them into the edges.

The quicksilver of his laugh.

The smell of his aftershave.

The beach. Salt and sand.

Pancake batter and maple syrup.

The warmth of his skin on yours. A flicker of his tongue.

Your own silent laughter—the kind that makes your eyes water and your stomach hurt. The pain is joyful.

A phone that rings and rings. Leaving faltering voicemails.

Wrap the box in tape until it feels like a brick. Stack other memories on top. Do not open the box, or even glance its way. Leave it for the cobwebs to gather. The more, the better.

Her Garden Is
By Nina Knueven

Her garden is marred with thorns
                     bristles of uneven shards threaten to
      pierce cellulose skins

         Her garden is a tapestry of overgrowth
            the hardened box enclosing its shape
perpetually fails
          —tendrils escape and scatter—
                 spiraling spreading dividing
           dartly blades of measured pastures

     Her garden is invaded with erroneous weeds
anguished with thirst
              thirst for her succulent strength
                  infest her roots
endeavor to choke new growth
              promising new sprouts

        Her garden is resilient
           voice only silenced for a season
   buries herself deep during droughts
awakening a reckoning

           breaking soil in the morning

        Her garden is colorful
  indulgent and lush
        lavishing crowned petals & ripe wilds
         natural orchestra coalesce
where bees bow their knees

Her garden is endangered
          Her garden is endowing
                    Her garden is thriving
          Her garden is a temple
                    Her garden is hers

It's Snowing in Mineola
By Clara Burghelea

I misremember you every so often
from the eyes to the touch then
it is the smell of you fading
like smoke across
lean waters.

And as I bow into their mirror
for a dash of such echoing,
the white of the garden
turns into dim light,
tall streetlamps
puncturing
the view.

Vapors of loss
breathe
in.

Selected Poems by Lorena Parker Matejowsky

Chapter One

1. In the beginning I was coarse
sand and above the ocean sending
starfish to the sky with only my
eyes. Who made me?
2. I remember walking on water
hauling a house full of hungry
leatherbacks behind.
3. Every step I struggled until they
emptied out the windows and
walked away. After that I had to
go under.
4. I was blistered in a barnacled
bathing suit but I sunk low and
slid around the sides until He let
me back in. Who knew this?
5. Every night I ached for an
anchor. Something to ground me
when the wet words would not
stop singing.
6. All I could do was knit nets to
hold my daughters down. Offer
Him amens. What happened?
7. In the end it didn't matter. I
swallowed the salt and softened to
stone, looking back at a ghost of
the Gulf all around me and
growing leaden legs.
8. Now I buoy the boys who drill
deep in the earth. My purpose
plateaued. I let their better feet
bruise my back to loose all that's
left.

9. My lap is for these laymen
fixed like me to something far
offshore.
10. Tonight I make myself an
island He can see from the
heavens.
11. Like a serpent fleeing Eden, I
forget it all.

I Have Questions:

If a mom falls out of bed at midnight who will hear it?
If she chokes will her children turn away from Youtubers
for two seconds? Will her husband help? If she screams
there's an alligator in the house will someone shake her
awake? If she asks for a raise and comes home angry
who will hush her howling? What will happen if she stops
showing up to teach Sunday School? Will the teen center
survive without her tithe? What if a man wants to walk
around her WalMart wearing a little black dress? What if
she pays for his pregnancy test? What if mom wants to
put out the campfire by pissing on it, too? Would her sons
stand by and watch? Could they learn something new
that day? What if the missing nativity scene from the
Austin County Courthouse appears in her attic? Who cares
about Confederate Heroes Day? Does Beth Moore have
a bible study on blasphemy? How do you get rid of
a hundred-year-old headache? When He calls us Home,
why can't our dogs come with us? What happens to women
who only embroider bad words? Do sins ever just show up
in your sewing basket? Would *Bitch* look better in blue
satin stich?

Having Fun

it's no big deal honey let me tell you what happened
to me at my first job and i turned out okay if a man
did that to me why i'd show him who's boss we all
know what happens when you've had one too many
lone stars and you're out after midnight honey it's
a man's world and it takes two to tango show me
a girl who hasn't had too many peach wine coolers and
regretted something the next day and i'll show you
your sunday school teacher taught that boy who ran
for bexar county judge didn't you go to school with
him and he spoke at our rotary meeting the other day what
a fine boy remember when you came home from that
party and we had to pick you up off the lawn lord you
kids were crazy how time flies when you were having
fun, weren't you?

Selected Poems by Brooke Lehmann

Trapped Wings
    for Stephen Copeland

Inside, after grieving for days,
I'm dreaming of how we store memories,
catch them like butterflies in a net.

Examine them, trap their tender wings
under braids of thread like captured
darlings, immobile, displayed at midday.

Where the sun shone bright over us
and I still desired my family, wanted
to cling to them like a dog with a bone.

Now, I'm inside a small apartment
while the dog sleeps and snores,
and I pass time like a monk.

A white butterfly floats by the window
fluttering to catch the sky, but
there is no sun here, just grey clouds

Rising in the horizon, a fresh sorrow pure
of knowing only because it's newly surfaced,
a few years old, my present wound.

I don't know how to release this truth,
so I capture it, disparage its wings,
in case, later, I don't remember.

On a Black Moon
after - Ada Limón

I take out my rage
And lay its knife

Under the pillow
Of broken dreams.

I light three candles
As a spell. One

For what could have been
Like dust around us

One for what will
Lift and carry

One for what will
Haunt and remind me—

We are its ghosts.

On The Frost Moon
Inspired by Alexander McQueen and Valerie Wallace

Fall's first frost shocks Seattle.

Beauty built her own house.

Others desire fickle fame, she wears

A blush bow to fan her flame.

Gravity's patterns always shift the tides

down her gentle silhouette.

But while she lives here in this body

sash, ruffle and lace gather

tender that is anything

but small. With time, reverie delights

as if a quiet petal falls, and leaves

wisdom beneath our translucent hands.

Selected Poems by Heather Lang-Cassera

Mourning Motherhood

Light spreads across the road
like butter being absorbed
into soft spaces.
This indulgence feels nothing,
disappears quietly.
Each time we drive this pass,
I think of all of the things
I should have said,
of the small sandwiches
I would have made
with and then
without the crust.

Loss Rekindled

I love you throws you every time.
I was never afraid of the dark—

but this, these flames of bereavement,
have no place inside a home.

You will not be able to count backward
to your final moments with her,

not to the metronome
of our stovetop clicking to light.

You do not need to say it.
I am not ready. I am not

ready, your absence

at breakfast tells me,

and this takes my breath away
as if all of the oxygen here,

in our place, is being
consumed by something else.

This Godless Grace

Imagine the lost
as the light that lapped up
our loved ones
allowing us to see
the curves of their bodies
before washing them clean
of this world.

That's a night outfit
By Margaret Reynolds

As soon as I arrive at camp, I know I hate Amber and her pink towel and her unsalted almond snacks.

Amber has long, blonde hair and an upturned nose that says, "I can do the splits. Can *you*?"

No Amber, I fucking can't.

While I haven't met Amber before, I've met Amber before. There's an Amber in my AP History class who's always asking me about scissoring. There's a boy Amber in gym class who still uses fag as a slur. (My working theory: He's stuck in a time loop in which he's reliving a domestic, 1950s period comedy over and over again.) And of course, the classic Amber — the Amber dads and teachers and nerds who like to call me *lady* and *she* even though we've had (like so many) conversations about pronouns. (LIKE SO MANY.)

So I hate Amber, and all I want to do is fart on her pillow.

So when Amber goes to the bathroom to brush her teeth, I fart on her pillow.

--

I've done an impressive job of avoiding Amber, and everything that she does and says. I get up before her. I never sit with her in the mess hall, and I avoid all water-based activities because those seem to be Amber's favorite.

(The last one's a huge bummer because I really, truly love swimming. But of course, Amber has taken this from me too.)

I'm considering spreading a rumor that Amber has some kind of water-born, flesh-eating virus but that feels a. mean (?) and b. easily disprovable given that Amber still has her flesh. Her stupid, pimple-free flesh.

--

Day four of camp and I end up in the same Friendship Bracelet Class as Amber.

Somehow (and by "somehow," I mean at the hands of a counselor who believes in "working with someone you haven't talked to yet"), Amber and I are made partners.

Amber: You're Elliana?

Me (no eye contact, grumpy dad voice): I go by El.

Amber: That's cool!

(What. A. Kiss. Up.)

Amber: So where are you from?

Me: North Carolina.

Amber: OMG SAME!

I cringe because Amber's normal voice could project across an auditorium, but her excited voice basically breaks the sound barrier.

Amber: Do you miss home?

Me (trying to think of emo lyrics to quote but instead coming up with the ever-witty...): No, it sucks.

Amber, nodding and chewing her lower lip: Yeah. Same... How do you like camp then?

I'm considering a few options at this point: fake diarrhea to go to the nurse (but then end up missing taco night, and everyone will think I have diarrhea), pretend Amber doesn't exist (but would this provoke Amber and all her Amber friends to engage in a quest of El's Destruction?), answer her (but I don't want to).

In the end, I shrug then proceed to silently make the dumb friendship bracelet, and though the counselor encourages us to "use multiple colors that represent your friend's personality and interests," I just use pink beads for Amber's.

Meanwhile, Amber makes me a friendship bracelet that has alternating green and black beads.

Amber (handing me the finished bracelet): It's because you are always playing capture the flag and getting green grass marks on your knees. And the black's because, uh, you like reading, and words in a book are black?

Amber (laughing nervously and suddenly quieter than usual): It's kind of silly.

Me (handing Amber her bracelet and suddenly feeling like a parent who stuffed their kid's Christmas stocking with oranges): Uh … You like pink, right?

She stares at her knees then, and while her cheeks maintain an even complexion, I realize when she tucks a strand of blonde behind her ear, that her lobes are bright red.

Me (without thinking): Your ears are blushing.

This makes Amber fully blush. I would have expected her cheeks to turn a perfect, animation bubblegum pink. Instead, red blotches creep over the tip of her nose, just under her bottom lip, across her left cheekbone.

Having been roundly mocked for the way my whole body turns red when I blush, I tense at the thought that maybe Amber thinks I'm making fun of her for the way that she blushes. (And while there are lots of things to make fun of Amber for doing, most involving wearing skirts to an ultimate Frisbee game, blushing is not one of those make-funable things.)

So I say: Don't worry. You're the only person I know who looks, uh, not ugly when they blush.

Then Amber laughs, and it's loud and round like church bells, but surprisingly, not in a bad way.

--

I go to taco night and get diarrhea, and while I'm binge eating calcium tablets in the nurse's office, I consider the possibility of not hating Amber. Let's be clear, I'm not going to *like* Amber. But maybe I could feel neutral towards Amber. Like Amber's a banana. Am I excited about bananas? No. They can be super mushy and gag-creating. Do I hate bananas? No. I'll take a banana in a banana-coffee smoothie every once in a while.

But then I return to our cabin and find that Amber has spearheaded the movement to call our cabin "Unicorn Lodge." Amber has also spearheaded a vote on this name, and without my dissenting opinion, "Unicorn Lodge" passed unanimously.

I find a glittery piece of construction paper bearing the name tacked to our cabin door, which confirms for me that Amber does not deserve a promotion to Banana. Amber is STILL an Amber. Amber will thus continue to be subject to my slow-as-to-make-more-demeaning eye rolls as well as my even slower, even louder sighs whenever she tells the cabin her story about meeting Prince Harry.

And to think I almost got fooled by a friendship bracelet.

--

Amber's gone to eat lunch, and I decide to steal her awful pink towel.

I have my own towel that I like a lot. I got it on a family vacation, and it features a map of Lake Tahoe with a period stain on the northern edge of the lake. I added the period stain after my mom complained about my baggy clothes. Also because I like when mothers at the beach wonder if maybe, possibly, I've murdered someone.

My period started this morning, and I've decided to add a matching period stain to Amber's towel. But when I pull it from her suitcase, guess what falls out?

C'mon, guess.

Here, we can play mad libs. (Out falls a baggy of _____ → insert noun).

(Our Amber ___ ___ →insert verb, insert noun)

(Our 6-pack, perfectly tanned Amber who is never (not once) been late to a camp activity, and just yesterday suggested we sing campfire songs around the campfire (are we 12?) ___ ___ →insert verb, insert noun)

(Our My-Favorite-Movie-Is-*Twilight* Amber ___ ___ →insert verb, insert noun)

Our Amber…

Smokes motherfucking* weed.

*Emphasis added by narrator.

--

I have the perfect blackmail. I've considered a number of ways to reveal this fact, but I have no access to blimps or any other necessary materials, so at lunch, without prelude, I say to Amber: I know you smoke weed.

Amber (looking left and right before hush whispering): What the fuck?

Me: I found weed in your towel.

Amber: Why did you have my towel?

Me (accidentally out loud): Shit.

Amber: Are you the one taking my stuff?

Me (Shrugging): …

Amber: Dude, that's so gross.

Me (blushing in my whole body kind of way): …

Amber (Sighing gently, sounding like a Belle who has gracefully spilled her tea. Gracefully in that the tea didn't spill on her dress or on carpet, just on the tile floor and thus can be wiped up easily): I didn't mean like *you're* gross. Just like, don't touch my stuff.

Me (Maybe experiencing a heat stroke): I'm really sorry about that.

Amber: Really, I don't think you're gross.

Me: It's totally fine.

Amber: You seem like a cool person.

Me: That's, uh, nice of you to say. You're a cool person too?

Amber: It's okay. I know you don't like me much…

Me (sounding as if I've inhaled helium out of a balloon): No I like you!!!!!

(There are that many exclamation marks in my voice. So many, in fact, that even Amber, who's quite fond of exclamation marks, jumps a little.)

Amber: …uh… okay…

Me: I don't like you, in like, a creepy way. I mean (starts laughing like an evil clown), I'm not going to murder you!!!! I mean (laughs like an even louder evil clown) I just don't know you that well!!!!

Amber (looking as if I've risen from the grave to talk to her): …

Me (feeling as if I've just risen from a grave, though not a grave on my home planet. Like I died and my body got transported to Mars and then I was raised from the dead and now I am forced to acclimate to life as an undead person operating within a foreign, literally alien, culture): …

Amber: Do you wanna go smoke some weed?

--

I end up stoned with Amber behind Cabin 12.

I feel stomach-weird because I hate Amber but I don't want her to know I hate her because I also have this deep-seated need to be liked, even if the person that likes me is a person I hate.

Also because Cabin 12 is a (*cough*) historical place.

(Cutaway to Australian/nature documentary-esque voiceover, overhead shot of Cabin 12.) Cabin 12 has an infamous history of drug usage, alcohol consumption, and (pause for dramatic effect) fornication. History textbooks note that Cabin 12 was the location where Jenny from the Princess Peach Cabin got fingered by Jordan Carmichael. History textbooks also report that Karen told Jenny who told this narrator that Alexander Orant licked Karen's left nipple behind Cabin 12. A number of visible specimens confirm these facts. (Zoom into a torn piece of red fabric.) Here we have a piece of Jenny's favorite cardigan, a classic byproduct of making out against rough tree trunks. (Zoom into a quarter.) Scientists have conducted a number of smell, feel, and warmth tests, and have concluded, without a doubt, that this quarter once resided in the back pocket of none other than Mr. Alexander Orant. However, the real mystery remains. (Zoom into used condom.) To whom does this belong?

Amber waits until her blue eyes are neatly lined with red to ask: Why don't you like North Carolina?

I'm not usually a chatty person, but weed has the ability to literally dry my tongue while metaphorically lubricating my tongue.

So I explain the North Carolina Amber problem, having enough social grace to not call my North Carolina enemies "Ambers."

Amber says: Yea, it's kind of the same for me.

Record scratch

Me: You?!

Amber: Everyone at my school was huge dicks when I came out as bisexual.

To which I numbly repeat: You?!

--

I've decided to not avoid the lake any longer—not because Amber suggested we kick all the straight boys out and make them "swim in kiddie pools as punishment for leering at our breasts as if they've never seen a mound of human tissue before."

--

We are laying on floaties during a free day when I unhappily notice Amber's dimples.

She floats toward me and says: So I heard this joke.

I say: Please don't.

She says: Knock, knock.

Me: I'm swimming away.

She continues: Who's there?

Me: I'm very politically against dad jokes.

Amber: Banana.

Me: I don't think you fully understand the irony of what's happening here.

Amber: Banana who?

Me (waiting for Amber to realize)

Amber: Aren't you glad I didn't say… Wait… I think I fucked up that joke.

--

The dimples have become a problem. They have encouraged me to smoke weed with Amber Not Once, Not Twice, but THRICE, now. THRICE.

It's on the third time that I get into the whole genderqueer, they/them pronoun thing, and Amber doesn't give me the "Why are you so weird?" Or "Why do you have to be so difficult?" or "That's just too hard for me to remember."

Amber gives me: Got it, dude.

And she gets it, dude.

--

Amber and I are swimming in the lake, and she's about fifteen strokes away from me when she yells to me: El! El, look at the sky! A rainbow! Isn't it pretty?

And a boy floating next to me says so only I can hear: God. She's such a ditz.

I look over at Amber, looking like a strawberry in a bright red-and-green one-piece, staring at the rainbow so intensely I become worried she'll look directly at the sun.

I get hot and say to the floating boy: Don't be a dick.

He laughs easily: You're one to talk.

--

I fully realize the extent of my dimple problem when Amber knocks knees with me at breakfast, and I freeze, a piece of half-chewed toast falling from my open mouth.

--

It's campfire night, and Amber and I go to the pool since no one will notice we are gone.

Me: I thought you loved campfire songs.

Amber: I fucking love campfire songs, but I just kind of feel like you will absolutely never sing a campfire song with me.

I closely examine a pinecone floating in the middle of the pool.

Still looking at the pinecone, I start: I would...

I pause, take a deep breath to force the words out, and end up inhaling a fly.

Amber: Are you okay?

Me (starting to cry because I am coughing that hard): I would sing *one* campfire song for you. But only one.

Amber's dimples appear, and I'm finally able to take a full, fly-free breath.

Amber: You would sing a campfire song *for me?*

Me: Don't be weird about it.

Amber (poking me under my ribs, giggling): You've come such a long way.

Me: Huh?

Amber: Since you used to hate me.

Me: I didn't hate you.

Amber: One time I asked you about your favorite mess hall meal, and you said, "Could you mind your own fucking business for once?"

Me: I just didn't like you.

Amber: But why?

Me: Well, it's just, uh, it's just you ate so many unsalted almonds.

Amber: … What?

Me: I thought I was being subtle. About hating you, I mean.

Amber: You absolutely were not.

Me (very quickly and loudly so I can't talk myself out of it): Well, I'm sorry.

Amber: For not telling me your favorite mess hall food? I mean, without knowing the definitive answer, I may spontaneously combust.

Me: I'm sorry for being mean to you. And thinking you're dumb because you like pink. I don't really get why you like pink. To me, it's objectively the worst color in that it's the color of boiled shrimp, which is the worst kind of shrimp.

Amber (narrowing her eyes): Have you tried boiled shrimp with cocktail sauce, though?

I continue: I also don't understand why you like unicorns but not horses. Because unicorns are just phallic horses. (I'm aware at this point that I'm rambling, but I am too afraid to look at Amber, having spent most of this speech staring at my yellowing, unpainted toenails, so I just fight onwards like the disgraced plastic toy soldier I very much feel like in this moment.) I don't really get you, but I like you. And I think you are funny and smart even though you like pink.

Amber (interjecting): Because I like pink.

Me (resisting the slow eye roll because I'm really trying for a genuine, Oscar-worthy apology here): Fine. You are funny and smart *because* you like pink. But that's not even the point, I guess. It's just… beyond it all. You were never mean to me, so I should have never been mean to you.

Amber: That was quite the speech.

Me: I'm sorry. About being mean. Also for the long speech.

Amber: You were a huge dick.

Me: I'm really sorry.

Amber: Like you have fully admitted to trying to smear period blood on my favorite towel.

Me: I maintain that period blood would improve your towel, but I am still very sorry for stealing it. And trying to blackmail you.

Amber: … You tried to blackmail me?

Me: Let's just focus on my apology.

Amber: I think I am going to need at least two campfire songs to get over this blackmail revelation.

Me (trying to get away from this campfire song business): Also, my favorite mess hall food is tacos.

Amber: Didn't they give you diarrhea?

Me: That's just the kind of relationship I have with my body.

--

Everyone else is asleep in the cabin when I look over to see a flashlight on under Amber's blanket.

I tiptoe across, scare her when I tap her knee and ask to crawl under the blanket.

I nod to the book under the flashlight's beam: What are you reading?

Amber (reading directly from the book): "He crawled into his friend's lap and found his friend's member was already hard, already ready."

Me: I thought you'd be reading unicorn books.

Amber: I also have some unicorn erotica. I could read you some.

Me (thankful that darkness covers up full-body blushing): So what happens after that dude crawls into his friend's lap?

--

So here's how things progress between Amber and me:

1. There's more knee-knocking under mess hall tables
2. There's a few pinky brushes on the way to the pool and one full hand hold during a relay race when Amber wants me to move faster (still counts)
3. Amber laying her head on my shoulder during the three (three!) campfire songs I agree to sing
4. Me commenting on Amber's floral skirt + floppy hat + ruffled white shirt for theater night, "That's a night outfit"

5. Amber commenting on my gym shorts and white t-shirt, "You look cute"

6. There's some note-passing. (Amber's very good at illustrating unicorns, and while I have problems with unicorns, I have generally positive feelings about her illustrations and notes, which always feature unicorns)

7. There's a lot more thigh touching and sitting close together

8. There's me having a dream in which I see Amber's nipples in a way that makes me feel quite creepy

Until—

--

We are back in the pool. It's another campfire night. We've fully gotten in, when Amber bites her lip, looks up at the sky, looks at me, looks back to the sky, and says to the moon, "I really like you."

Me (because Amber's looking at the moon, so I decide to go for a dad joke in which I'm pretending to be the moon, and Amber's talking to the moon, so I imitate what I think would be a moon voice): I really like you too, Amber.

Amber: What voice was that?

Me: Never mind.

Amber: You like me too?

Me: But not in a creepy, murder you kind of way.

Amber: … What about in a kiss me kind of way?

She says this while looking at the tip of my nose, so I look at the tip of her nose.

I say: The tip of your nose is blushing.

And then I realize, that if I'm not going to miss kissing the indent of Amber's crescent dimples, and if I'm not going to let Amber look at me like I'm the tastiest of tater tots that she both wants to eat but is also a little afraid that me (the tater tot) may be poisonous…

I realize nothing because before I can get to the end of this thought, Amber kisses me.

And then pulls away very quickly, so I tuck a piece of hair behind her ear, her very red ear, and kiss her back.

She tastes like popcorn. Homemade stove popcorn and bad horror movies and worn living room couches. It's definitely not a dry kiss, but there's no saliva bridges, for which I'm grateful.

I kiss each of her dimples. I kiss her hairline, which smells like Garnier Fructis. I kiss a blush on the edge of her chin.

She presses into me, kisses every blush she can find on my face and my neck, which is to say—everywhere.

I break away from her only when I hear screaming, but she holds me close, her hand cupped around the back of my neck.

Amber: It's only the cicadas, she murmurs into my collarbone.

Me (pulling away slightly): That doesn't feel like a good sign.

Amber: It's what cicadas are supposed to do. You know, like, they live underground forever. Then they come up and shed their skins. I feel like the screaming is, like, a celebration of freedom.

She kisses me again, pulling my lower lip between hers. She smells like chlorine.

Me (being not good at this kissing thing, pulls away again): Don't cicadas die right afterward though?

Amber: Don't think about that. Think about the freedom. It's like a metaphor, you know? How you've come out of your shell in this story.

Me: Wait, I'm in a stor—

Contributors:

Cover Artist:

Letisia Cruz is a Cuban-American writer and artist. She is the author of *The Lost Girls Book of Divination* (Tolsun Books). Her chapbook, *Chonga Nation* was selected as a finalist in the 2018 Digging Press Chapbook Series and the 2016 Gazing Grain Chapbook Contest. Her writing and artwork have appeared in *[PANK]*, *Ninth Letter*, *The Acentos Review*, *Gulf Stream*, and *300 Days of Sun*, among others. She is a graduate of Fairleigh Dickinson University's MFA program and lives in Florida with her partner and their two cats. Find more of her work at lesinfin.com.

Inspiration for "Vive La Resistance"

My illustrations are rendered primarily in pen and ink on paper. I am inspired by strong, trailblazing women who push boundaries, forge their own paths, and define for themselves what it means to achieve success. I am also inspired by the take-no-shit attitude of the 1990s and transformative self-expression made possible through art, poetry and music. My work often depicts tattooed women straddling light and dark, gazing into their own abyss, and defining their sense of self. Much of my work is infused with elements of nature and centered around the seasons, the passing of time, and the theme of rebirth.

Jennifer Battisti is a Las Vegas native. She won "Best Local Writer" by readers of Desert Companion (2019). Her chapbook, Echo Bay, was released in 2018 (Tolsun Books). Her work has appeared in or is forthcoming from *Manzano*

Mountain Review, Thin Air Magazine, Coe Review, and *The Briar Cliff Review*.

Clara Burghelea is a Romanian-born poet with an MFA in Poetry from Adelphi University. Recipient of the Robert Muroff Poetry Award, her poems and translations appeared in *Ambit, HeadStuff, Waxwing, The Cortland Review* and elsewhere. Her collection, *The Flavor of The Other,* is scheduled for publication in 2020 with Dos Madres Press. She is the Translation/International Poetry Editor of *The Blue Nib.* Find her on Instagram at @clara_burghelea and Twitter: @ioanaclara.

Winner of Orison Books' 2018 Anthology Short Story Award, **Lawrence Cady** has published works in journals such as *Other Voices, South 85 Journal, The Literary Review, Natural Bridge, Portland Review, Red Rock Review, Cream City Review, Roanoke Review, South Dakota Review*, and others. A graduate of University of Wisconsin–Madison and Portland State University, Cady has served as managing editor for the peer-reviewed science journal Astrobiology (Mary Ann Liebert, Inc., New Rochelle, NY) from 2002 to the present.

Diana L. Conces writes poetry and fiction from her home in the Texas Hill Country. Over seven dozen of her poems have appeared in print and online publications, on a bus, and in a newspaper. She is the author of a novel, *The Golden Feather* and a poetry chapbook, *Blue Skies & Blacktop*. She blogs at dianalconces.blogspot.com and is on Instagram at @dianaconces.

Jenna Dirksen is a senior at the University of Tennessee studying creative writing. Her poetry has been published by *Z Publishing, Grlsplain*, and the University of Tennessee's historic, *Phoenix Magazine*. She is currently the poetry section editor for *Phoenix Magazine* and hopes to continue working in publishing after graduation. Find her on Instagram: @croco_diles.

Jen Drake holds an MA in English Education from SUNY College at Cortland. When she's not writing, gardening, or wandering the hills and gorges of the southern Finger Lakes with her dog, she trains and supervises online tutors and serves in her union. She has previously published work in *Raquette Lake News*.

Jeannine Hall Gailey served as the second Poet Laureate of Redmond, Washington. She's the author of five books of poetry: *Becoming the Villainess, She Returns to the Floating World, Unexplained Fevers, The Robot Scientist's Daughter*, and *Field Guide to the End of the World*, winner of the Moon City Press Book Prize and the SFPA's Elgin Award. She's also the author of PR for Poets: A Guidebook to Publicity and Marketing. Her work appeared or will appear in journals such as *American Poetry Review, Ploughshares*, and Poetry. Her website is www.webbish6.com. You can find her on Twitter and Instagram: @webbish6.

Lisa Gaudio is a current MFA student, writer, and poet located in New Haven, CT. Her work has been published in *Helix Literary Magazine, Zines + Things, Hartford Courant*, and *The Apeiron Review*. In 2015, she was nominated as a student poet in the CT Poetry Circuit.

Bree Devones Hsieh was born on the West Coast, raised in the Dakotas, and lives in the Los Angeles area. Her poems appear or are forthcoming in *Blue Unicorn, I-70 Review, Dappled Things, Piltdown Review, Chaleur Magazine*, and *Sojourners Magazine*.

Seth Jani lives in Seattle, WA and is the founder of Seven CirclePress (www.sevencirclepress.com). Their work has appeared in *The American Poetry Journal, Chiron Review, The Comstock Review, Ghost City Review, Rust+Moth* and *Pretty Owl Poetry*, among others. Their full-length collection, *Night Fable*, was published by FutureCycle Press in 2018. Visit them at www.sethjani.com.

Nina Knueven's work has appeared in *The White Wall Review, Heavy Feather, River River, SOS Art, Nexus*, and elsewhere. She lives in Cincinnati with her family where she tutors, edits, and writes poetry.
Find her on Instagram at:
www.instagram.com/niiinnnnnaaaaa.

Heather Lang-Cassera is the Clark County, Nevada Poet Laureate. She holds a Master of Fine Arts in Poetry with a Certificate in Literary Translation. Her poems have been published by *december, Diode, The Normal School, North American Review, Paper Darts, Pleiades, South Dakota Review*, and many other literary journals, and they have been on exhibit in the Nevada Humanities Program Gallery and elsewhere. She has been awarded project and professional development grants from the Nevada Arts Council and serves as a world literature editor and literary critic for *The Literary Review*, faculty advisor for *300 Days of Sun*, literary critic for *Reading in Translation*, and editor-in-chief for Tolsun Books. At Nevada State College, Heather teaches Introduction to Creative Writing, World Literature II, Modern American Poetry, and more. Find her at: www.heatherlang.cassera.net or on Instagram/Twitter: @Heather__Lang__.

Emily Larkin is an Australian author and academic, and holds a Doctor of Creative Arts (Creative Writing) from the University of the Sunshine Coast. She is the author of The *Whirlpool*, a picture book about a polar bear's journey through life's highs and lows. *The Whirlpool* is illustrated by Helene Magisson and published by Wombat Books. Emily writes short fiction for teens and adults -- and her work has been published in Australian and international literary journals. Emily loves sharing a passion for writing by running creative workshops at the Queensland Writers Centre. She also tutors in Creative Writing and Communication at The University of Queensland, and the Queensland University of Technology International College. To follow Emily, visit https://www.facebook.com/ehlarkinauthor/.

Brooke Lehmann is a poet currently living in Seattle, WA. She received her B.S. in Chemical Engineering from Purdue University and sees poetry as a form of engineering meaning with words. She began writing through her recovery with chronic illness. Outside of writing, she also enjoys fashion modeling, kettlebells and restorative yoga. Find more info at brookelehmann.com or on Instagram: @blehmann524.

R. Nikolas Macioci earned a PhD from The Ohio State University, and for thirty years taught for the Columbus City Schools. In addition to English, he taught Drama and developed a Writers Seminar for select students. OCTELA, the Ohio Council of Teachers of English, named Nik Macioci the best secondary English teacher in the state of Ohio. Nik is the author of two chapbooks: *Cafes of Childhood* and *Greatest Hits*, as well as seven books: *Why Dance, Necessary Windows, Cafes of Childhood* (the original chatbook with additional poems), *Mother Goosed, Occasional Heaven, A Human Saloon*, and *Rustle Rustle Thump Thump*. Critics and judges called *Cafes of Childhood* a "beautifully harrowing account of child abuse," but not "sentimental" or "self-pitying," an "amazing book," and "a single unified whole." *Cafes of Childhood* was submitted for the Pulitzer Prize in 1992. In addition, more than two hundred of his poems have been published in the US and abroad in magazines and journals, including The SOCIETY OF CLASSICAL POETS Journal, *Chiron, Concho River Review*, and *Blue Unicorn*.

He won First Place in the 1987 National Writer's Union Poetry Competition, judged by Denise Levertov; First Place in The Baudelaire Award Competition, sponsored by The World Order of Narrative and Formalist Poets (1989); Second Place in Zone 3's first annual Rainmaker Awards, judged by Howard Nemerov (1989); and Second Place in the Writer's Digest annual competition, judged by Diane Wakoski (1991).

Lorena Parker Matejowsky is a resident of Central Florida but spent her first thirty years in Texas. Her poetry was selected for the 2018 AWP Intro Journal Prize and *Best New Poets 2018* anthology. She received an MFA in Creative Writing from the University of Central Florida. Fin her on Twitter: @LorieMatejowsky.

Ollie McLean is a Florida-born writer currently based in Queens, N.Y. Her work explores many facets of femininity with a lens for nontraditional family dynamics, and it is often steeped in the wildness of her Florida upbringing. After spending her first professional years in the classroom, she is excited to focus wholly on writing and her journey into publication. She is currently an MFA candidate in fiction at Adelphi University. You can follow her on Instagram: @olliepips and Twitter: @OliviaMc89.

Madeline Miele currently lives in Portland, Maine. Her work has appeared in *Dogwood: A Journal of Poetry and Prose*, *The Stonecoast Review*, and *Uppagus*.

Terry Minchow-Proffitt lives in St. Louis, MO. His poems have appeared in numerous journals and magazines. His chapbook, *Seven Last Words* (2015), as well as the collections *Chicken Train: Poems from the Arkansas Delta* (2016) and *Sweetiebetter* (2019), were published by Middle Island Press.

His poetry, essays, and other occasional musings can be found at www.terryminchow-proffitt.com.

Arjun Parikh's work has appeared in *Mud Season Review*, *Into the Void Magazine*, and *phoebe*. He graduated from New York University in 2018 and will begin law school in August. He lives in Palo Alto, California, where he teaches middle schoolers and writes.

Margaret Reynolds is a genderqueer writer based in Colorado. They write queer romances with a sprinkle of ghost and drink copious amounts of iced coffee like all card-holding bisexual vampires. You can find more of their work at margaret-reynolds.com. Find Margaret on Twitter: @thatmountaingay.

Thank you for reading! Stay in touch:

www.blackfoxlitmag.com
Website

www.facebook.com/blackfoxlit
Facebook

@blackfoxlit
Twitter & Instagram

www.blackfoxlitmag.com/contact/
Newsletter

Check out some of our previous issues:

Find more of our issues at blackfoxlitmag.com!

Resources for Writers from BFLM Editor Racquel Henry's Writer's Atelier:

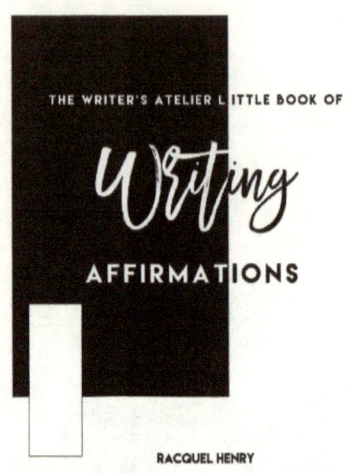

The Writer's Atelier Little Book of Writing Affirmations

The Complete Revision Workbook for Writers

www.ingramcontent.com/pod-product-compliance
Lightning Source LLC
Chambersburg PA
CBHW050832180626
46814CB00004B/1574